PEOPLE
AND DOG
IN THE SUN

People
and
Dog
in the
Sun

Ronald Wallace

University of Pittsburgh Press

Published by the University of Pittsburgh Press, Pittsburgh, Pa. 15260
Copyright © 1987, Ronald Wallace
All rights reserved
Feffer and Simons, Inc., London
Manufactured in the United States of America

Library of Congress Cataloging in Publication Data

Wallace, Ronald.
  People and dog in the sun.

  (Pitt poetry series)
  I. Title. II. Series.
PS3573.A4314P4   1987   811'.54   86–25041
ISBN 0-8229-3552-X
ISBN 0-8229-5388-9 (pbk.)

Some of these poems have originally appeared in the following publications: *Abraxas* ("Secrets"); *American Poetry Review* ("Sinbad the Sailor"); *Cedar Rock* ("Assembling," "Nightline," and "Seaside, Cozumel"); *Chariton Review* ("The Magician's Lunch"); *The Chowder Review* ("People and Dog in the Sun"); *Images* ("Constipation"); *Kayak* ("Old Times"); *New Letters* ("Well"); *North American Review* ("At Half-Moon Bay"); *Northeast* ("The Worrier"); *Poet & Critic* ("Trash-picking"); *Poetry Northwest* ("The Anatomy of the Hand," "Bat," "Geography," "Poem Written Mostly by Fourth-Graders," "The Poetry Lesson," "Softball," and "Words, Words"); *Prairie Schooner* ("Grouse" and "Poppies"); *Quarterly West* ("Merida: The Market"); *Rubicon* ("Ground Zero"); *Southern Poetry Review* ("Bingo" and "Who Art in Heaven"); *Sou'wester* (" 'Welcome to the Only Waunakee in the World' "); *Tar River Poetry* ("Matheny"); *Wisconsin Academy Review* ("The Juggler" and "Morels"); *The Wooster Review* ("The Secret of Levitation"); *Yankee* ("This Night"); and *Yarrow: A Journal of Poetry* ("Fencing" and "Long for this World").

Most of the poems in the first section were originally published as a chapbook, *The Owl in the Kitchen* (Meadville, Pa.: Heatherstone Press, 1985). Special thanks to Jeanne Braham.

I would also like to thank the Wisconsin Arts Board (in conjunction with the National Endowment for the Arts), the Graduate School Research Committee of the University of Wisconsin, and the Wisconsin Foundation (with a grant from Norman Bassett) for their generous support.

The publication of this book is supported by grants from the National Endowment for the Arts in Washington, D.C., a Federal agency, and the Pennsylvania Council on the Arts.

For Peggy, Molly, and Emily

Also by Ronald Wallace

Poetry
Plums, Stones, Kisses & Hooks, 1981
Tunes for Bears to Dance To, 1983

Poetry Chapbooks
Installing the Bees, 1977
Cucumbers, 1977
The Facts of Life, 1979
The Owl in the Kitchen, 1985

Criticism
Henry James and the Comic Form, 1975
*The Last Laugh: Form and Affirmation in the Contemporary American
    Comic Novel,* 1979
God Be with the Clown: Humor in American Poetry, 1984

CONTENTS

CONTENTS

I. The Owl in the Kitchen

MORELS

Ten years of abuse and neglect—
the pastures gone to boulders and weeds,
a fury of dandelions and wild mustard,
the sheds and pole barn wrecked,
the farm house filled with old postcards and feces—
has brought us here in this dry heat
hoping to change our lives.

I complain there is too much to do,
there is simply nothing for us
in this unfamiliar country
we've grown so apart from.
But you are off in a clatter of crows,
scavenging the scrub woods,

and I follow, lashed by brambles and prickly ash,
past oak stumps and sumac,
the hot sun ablister with poison ivy and ticks,
until, lost now, seeing nothing,
I scree down the deep gully and out,
stone-cut and root-torn, to reach

this cool knoll, rich with hackberry,
aspen, and walnut, the moist understory
matted with leaves, where I see,
popping up from the dark earth as I watch them,
columbine, wood violets, bellwort, morels,
and you, your arms full of strange
penises, champagne corks, found money.

WOODCOCKS

All spring they've been comically
peenting their foolish kazoos,
then thrumming like buzz bombs
skyward to dusk
in godlike invisible circles,
just to fall back to the grass
and their goofy complaints:
Peent! Peent!

You wonder: if our love required
this kind of boast and abasement
would we be here tonight
on this grassy knoll
overlooking the April woodcocks?
Peent! I call out to you,
circling your lips,
my heart ridiculously thrumming.

THE NUDE GARDENER

Surrounded by burdock and foxtail
on the hillside behind the house
you dig up a would-be garden,
nude except for your shoes.

Inside, I watch your breasts swing
as you bend to your work,
your buttocks slightly puckered
with strain and middle age.

Your leg to the spade, your hand
shading your eyes, you gaze
somewhere into the far trees
and smile. What do you see?

Is it the neighboring farmer
falling off his tractor in amazement?
The mailman on his rural rounds
handed a package he'll deliver

to every friend in town?
The farmer's son, fourteen, coon
hunting, as he's told his mom
every day this week?

Or is it something farther off,
more ancient than the trees,
that tingles on your skin
and makes my married knees

weaker with anticipation
than for years they've been?
Weeds fall off the hillside
and you are standing in

coneflower, hollyhock, bergamot,
blossoming with wild abandon!

THE OWL IN THE KITCHEN

For days we'd been exclaiming
over scuffling in the ductwork,
wondering what shape
our speculations would take.
Now, here in the kitchen,
he's smaller than we'd have expected,
his beak curved toward confusion,
his wise eyes blindered with light,
hooked to the top of the freezer
as if he might be mistaken
for an oven mitt, or feather duster.

We open the doors and windows,
letting November inside,
and then the whole kitchen's a bluster,
a windstorm of feathers and wings,
the cat growing fat, a soprano
lifting her voice to sing,
the children, feathered with wonder,
careening off ceiling and walls,
the whole stunned kitchen giddy,
all moony eyes and claws,

and then he's gone,
leaving us only ourselves
and a breakfast of morning light.
And this family for whom, unbidden,
blessings pause in their flight.

LONG FOR THIS WORLD

All night the spring peepers rasp and trill
their lovemaking into song. In the clear
morning light, the pond glistens with pearl
strands strung from the cress and willow.
The old granary's ticking, about to go off
with cardinal and chickadee and swallow.

Today you are twelve. Last night,
you tell us, you dreamed us all dead,
our bodies cracked open and empty as shells.
Now all day you see death in the plum
blossoms dropping, the woodpecker's hollow
chortle and knock, the long grass's ravishing.

You beg us please never to leave you,
never to die. We won't, we lie,
and you believe it. But your body, aching
to replace us, good fledgling, good frog,
starts up its own secret trilling, unpinning
the pearly grenades of its song.

GROUSE

Scything brambles and prickly ash, high on
the hillside deer trail, I flush a grouse.
Six chicks skitter up over the razorback ridge
while the mother dances madly in the underbrush.
Before I can assure her I mean her no harm,
I've come down with the brush scythe and bagged her
in some preverbal instinctual rush
and there's grouse on a fire spit for dinner.

When I come back to myself, making my pale explanations,
she'll have none of it. Rigid with outrage and terror,
a display of fanned wings and tail feathers,
a russet and ocher squawk in the awkward brush,
she escorts me tersely fifty yards up the trail
before exploding like a motor in my heart.

BAT

When you slide open the barn door
the bat drops from the sky like a rag
or a hand, and lands on your back,
wings spread. The day holds its breath,
the sunlight turns hard, a glare.

We're all in a photograph, the shutter
clicked down on the overexposed moment:
you, half-turned toward the barn;
the children, stopped midstride
between anticipation and fear;
me, fixed in my bare hands and feet.
Meanwhile, the bat,
webbed with leather and fur, has turned
his small head back and is hissing,
something about razors and surprise.

And then everything quickens: my swift
hand, the air, the sunlight, our voices
fly out of the frame, leaving
that small piece of ourselves behind,
flat in the high grass, undeveloped,
a shadow among thistles and nettles.

FENCING

Someone's been cutting the trees in our woods,
leaving the blunt stumps to fester in brush,
the piles of lopped limbs and snapped branches
groping toward brambles of light.

When he sees me coming, he kills the chain saw
and puts forth a pudgy hand, smiling.
His voice, all whine and tinsel,
is strangely too high for his bulk.

Before I know it, he's got me by the ears,
his voice sawing off all my objections.
He says he's just cut some dead elms and brush,
thrusting his stumpy finger a good fifty yards

up our hill. He's putting up line fence—
this dead wood, these obstructions,
they all gotta go. You don't mind, he says.
Gotta make room for the truck.

I watch our property diminish,
our trees fall word by word,
hauled out on the winch of his voice.
Although he's a whole head shorter than I,

somehow, I feel small, fragile,
my own hand a thin twig in his grasp.
I'm new to the country, a poet, a joke
in the Bear Valley Bar, but

I beg to differ, I say. I'm sorry, excuse me.
For me it's walnuts and birches;
for him, it's obstructions and brush.
He's no farmer, I think. He's a miner.

He waits, logging all my objections.
The old fence line extends in the distance, stumped,
the box elders cut off at the ankles.
Night seeps in like an oil spill,

the sky a scattered sawdust of stars.
In the back of the truck, his ten-year-old son
bends to the wind of his voice,
his disked eyes vacant, clear-cut.

And they're off in a rumble of worn shocks and rust,
leaving me on this thin line between anger and grief,
the ridge stretching off in the distance
like a regret. Late that night I dream

of them, swollen out of all proportion,
rolling over hillside after hillside,
trees snapping like so many pencils,
stacked up like reams of new paper.

And I'm running my lines around them,
my voice full of barbed wire and steel,
singing the seedlings and sap up,
fencing, fencing for real.

THE CINEMATICS OF LOSS

A man's family leaves on a trip to Idaho.
He drives them out to the station
at Columbus, Wisconsin, where the train
barely stops, just slows down and lets them on
and then speeds up again and is gone
before he's even noticed. He had planned
to get on that train and examine
the seats, take care of the luggage, fluff
the pillows, with hugs and kisses around.
He would have given his two children
spending money to remember him by,
and told his wife he loved her, after all.
But they're gone.
The tracks are gray and filled with rain,
and he's a stranger in this small town.

Later, on the ridge behind his house,
looking at the oak tree he built steps onto
for the children, he imagines he is
the director of a film about loss,
and the lead character, and the audience sitting down.
He looks at the tree and sees through a mist
the superimposed ghost figures of his children,
the sound of their echoing laughter,
and then there is only the sound of the wind,
and the trees, and the rain, and the tears on his face
streaming down. Did the train crash in the night?
Was no one heard from again? Did the man grow
old in his young family's dying?
No. It was only a movie.

His family comes back as if nothing
has happened, right on schedule,
the day bright and slow and immortal.
But no matter how hard he tries not to
he goes through his life
thinking somehow they're all still in Idaho.
Somehow they're no more than a flat flicker of light,
a half-finished reel that will end, as it must,
in some theater of loss, with its own train of thought,
in the rain, in the dark, without any of them.

THIS NIGHT

Seated beside them,
squeezing the rubbery teats,
breathing to the ping of the milk stream,
I can almost forget
how anyone could want
anything other than this:
the horses shifting softly in the stalls,
the eight cats arranged politely
around the tin of skimmed-off milk,
the nubians on their regal platforms,
queens of the field and feed bin.

Until I dream the whole world eating,
the universe dreamily eating,
as, under the hungry stars,
the night closes its great beak,
and a barn owl's wheezy shriek
detonates the light,
as if this were the last night
for us all,
and not just any night.

AT CHET'S FEED & SEED

The man who is telling me about the chicken
stationery he makes in his backyard trailer
leaves with his beaky wife.
Their voices clabber and scratch.
In the corner, guinea hens, $1.50 each,
scutter and strut in jerky grandeur.
Clyde is pleased to meet me. He
shakes my hand, a 200 lb. feed bag
perched on his left shoulder, his big
arm, glistening in its sleeveless T-shirt,
a mixture of roast corn, oats, molasses, wheat.
The bald woman tied up to her chihuahua,
her son still in Vietnam with the marines,
adjusts her rheumy teeth.
She says he'll be coming back.
Chet says he will, pulls a pencil out of his ear
and takes a dollar off her bill.
She grunts. Chet bleats at Clyde
who whinnies under the weight of the feed sack.
The chicken man and his wife come back.
They're looking at me.
The smell of feed and goodwill is sweet.
I feel so stupid I could almost moo
with approval. So I do.

II. Words, Words

WORDS, WORDS

Why is it I always love best
what I cannot see—
the children with their affectionate
nattering, the old house
with its cracked siding and broken door,
you with all your various perfections?
Why is it this loveliness I dream of
vanishes in the thunder of familiarity and use?
So that even now, at this very moment,
faced with all this good life holds for me,
I'm thinking of some love I once threw over—
the sherry of her hair, the glint of
sunlight in her eye,
the sweet words enrapturing my tongue.

CONSTIPATION

Stuck each summer at Bible camp
with the ten-year-old wits and prophets,
I would not be
the victim of hoots and whistles,
the object of chortles and leers.
I knew the body was holy.
So, chary of farts and gasses,
I squeezed it back all week,
and learned the proper responses:
He who smelt it, dealt it;
A skunk can't smell his own stink.

Until one night,
cramped up and desperate,
I sneaked out to the latrine,
and there saw Sally Harper,
immaculate in the moonlight,
angelic as a dream,
slide through the forbidden door
as the night filled with her
blats, toots, grunts, and raspberries.
And then I laughed myself silly,
and knew what a heaven was for.

OLD TIMES

He calls at ten; doesn't have a date again
and wants to come over. I remember
the back seat of his '59 Lincoln, equipped
with television, phone, booze, women,
and the long hot nights of adolescence.
Yes, I hear myself say, from somewhere far away.

My wife rolls her eyes, goes home
to her mother forever. I forget her.
Our house grows larger, fills up
with my sisters and brothers. King Richard returns
to the air, playing requests: the Chordettes,
Richy Valens, Buddy Holly, the Big Bopper.

I get drunk, waiting, cigarettes and rubbers
stashed under my jacket. I am big stuff,
smiling into my glass. Sixty seasons pass.
He knocks on the door, big as a bear,
belly full of beer. Suddenly, I grow older, decades
sprouting from my chin. But I wave him on in.

He has not changed: I do not recognize him.
Without hesitation, he rips off my beard,
breaks my pale head in his hard fist,
flips the collar of my white shirt up, says I'll be
fine. Suddenly, it's only nine. I sit in the corner
smiling, as he finishes with my sister.

MATHENY

Remember me? The class jack-off.
In ninth grade I ripped up
a whole row of bolted down school desks
and threw them out the music room window.
You applauded. You egged me on. I'd do
everything you wanted to but wouldn't:
throb spitwads at the teacher,
snap any girl's bra strap,
blow farts on my naked arm.

M'weenie! you called out. *M'weenie!*

I took the heat, paid the piper, faced
the music, while you,
getting your rocks off, looked on.
Now who's the failure? You
with your teacup hands,
your bald smiles and small promotions?
Or me, Matheny, the flunky, the great
debunker. Your drab imagination's ingot.
The gold in your memory's coffer.

THIRTEEN

Gent, Nugget, Swank, and *Dude:*
the names themselves were lusty, crude,
as I took my small detour from school,
my breath erect, my manner cool.

In Kranson's Drugstore, furtive, alert,
stiff in my khakis I'd sneak to the back,
unzip the new issue from its thick stack,
and stick it in my quick shirt.

Oh, I was a thief for love,
accompliced by guilt and thrill,
mystery and wonder my only motive.

Oh, that old Kranson could be there still!
I'd slip in and out, liquid, unseen,
out of my mind again, thirteen.

GEOGRAPHY

She wore her knowledge
like a proof of my stupidity.
Though it has been years,
today when I see her again,
bedridden, blank, and secret
as the teacher's manual
we'd never see,
I am back at the blackboard,
throat thick with chalk, tongue
dusty with all the wrong answers.

She knew where the conifers and broadleafs,
which rivers and oceans,
whose limestone and wheatcrop,
what years of loss and abundance,
why this city, that town.
She knew that I'd never
know the right answers—
which place in the country
the highest, the lowest,
which type of strata how strong.

But now as she lies there
still as a fact, dumbfounded,
her heart all thumbs,
I want to tell her
exactly how I got along,
traveling different landscapes,
learning the geography of song.
And if she says bedrock,
Mount McKinley, Death Valley,
I'll know that this time she's wrong.

THE ANATOMY OF THE HAND

Consider, she says, all the things
you could not do without hands.
And while she's appraising
the buttons and stays,
the feeding and hygiene,
the doorknobs and levers and drawers,
I'm watching handfuls of words fall away
into the lackluster cadaver bin
with all the amputated phrases:
grasp, snatch, hold, caress, and fondle,
touch, finger, fist, punch, and feel,
squeeze, clutch, grip, slap, and tickle,
heaped up with the glad hands,
the high hands, the upper hands,
the in hands, and out of hands,
even hands, under hands . . .

Meanwhile, the hands,
stiff on their meaty limbs,
yellow and waxen,
the skinned tendons splayed back
to display the conjunction
of nerve end and jointure,
tensor and flexor,
phalange and digit,
the synovial sheaths,
the cutaneous circulation,
the horned fingernails
ordinary as corn,
the crabbed fingers bending
to fend off or fondle,
reaching up from their silvery tray,
say nothing.

She's talking with her hands,
she who would be
the perpetual wallflower—
studious, friendless, lost
in her glasses and splotchy complexion,
her mumble and stringy hair,
her pimples and shapeless frame—
while her hands,
delicate in their precision,
flash in the air, flutter and rush,
bloom and maneuver and swim through
the endless movements
of navicular, lunate, triangular, and pisiform,
her carpal diagrams and charts.

I imagine late hours at the anatomy lab,
alone with the hands
reaching up toward her, cradled
as if she were reading what's left
of their palms, or casually doing
their nails, or just holding on,
her own hands glistening with
acetic acid or sweat
to loosen the movement,
the last one asked to dance,
gently stroking the hands,
attentive to every nerve end and fiber,
every involuntary signal and twitch,
the hands, reaching, stretching,
the hands in her lap turning, dancing,
the hands saying nothing
in a language all their own.

ASSEMBLING

I spread the parts out on the driveway,
checking for Belt A, Loop C,
Bottom Seating Pad, Hook Side Latch,
Self-Locking Washers and Nuts, wondering
why there are always too few parts
or too many, as I bolt Clamp B on
upside down and backwards, hoping
no one will stop by to watch.

I remember Billy Elson's older brother,
gimp-legged and grinning,
following us around the house,
friendly and gentle as a pup.
We called him "Loony," but
armed with the crudest of diagrams,
thick glasses, and Duco Cement,
he could put the 1000 tiny pieces
of a Testor's plastic model
into the proper holes and slots
and come up with
U-boats, aircraft carriers, destroyers,
more perfect than the pictures on the box.
Until one day with his father's shot-
gun, he blew them all back into pieces,
and Billy, and himself, and his father,
leaving us and his mother in shock.
No one could put it together.

And now, here at the flanged end
of late middle age, I find myself

rattled by the simplest instructions,
looking for the Support Straps,
Safety Valves, and Protective Housings,
surrounded by boxes of half-finished projects,
knowing I won't bring anything to perfection,
won't finish anything up.

THE MAGICIAN'S LUNCH

—for Dave

The audience is skeptical, expecting tricks.
He tries hard to please them,
works with his rings, wands, and knots.
They yawn. He thinks: What do they want?
He tries harder, shows them his empty
sleeves and boxes, gives them his coins and cards.
They grow restless, begin
to mutter and complain. They're bored,
they want something more. They think
with the right words he could walk on water,
lie on nails, escape from all cells and locks.
But he's given them all he's got,
and simple as sleight of hand, they're gone.
Alone on stage, he sighs, thinks about lunch.
From behind his right ear
he pulls out an egg
that sprouts wings and flies away.
From under his handkerchief
he conjures up water that flares up
flame red, then black, then ash gray.
Now he's starving, he's famished.
Each flank steak he saws in half
grows back together
before he can lift up his fork.
Whole sides of beef disappear up his sleeves
and bread levitates out of reach
until he's so hungry he's weak.
Now the audience returns, applauding.
They laugh as he pulls strings of hot dogs
from his pockets: dachshunds
that run yapping away. They cheer as he grabs at

roast turkeys that vanish, succulent
ducks and rabbits swallowed up by his hat.
Now his stomach's in knots, hunger
twisting its tight rings inside him.
Thin as a wand, he rolls into his handkerchief,
folds up and blows away.
Now the audience, astonished,
suckled with wonder, reverent as prayer,
takes one breath and rises, fat with applause,
ovations and encores gorging the sated air,
while across America,
hard before mirrors, nothing to lose,
disciples are dieting,
spreading their thin good news.

SOFTBALL

On the mound the pitcher twirls the ball.
He's drunk, his beer propped in the dust.
I'm at the plate, wondering if I'm too old
for this game. Out in the field
the tanned adolescents, barefoot in the grass,
are having a high old time.

The umpire signals it's time
to start. The pitcher screws up the ball
and lets fly. I glance out at the grass
and swing, as the ball falls into the dust.
The infielders chatter, "Hey, old
man, you don't belong on this field,

maybe you should try some other field,
engineering perhaps?" The next time
the pitch comes, I take it—the old
"wait 'em out" ploy. I'm on the ball
now, I'll leave those youngsters in the dust.
Let them stand in the field and chew grass.

Years ago, though, it seemed that the grass
was greener. I remember the Ohio field
where we lay in the alfalfa and dust
and made love for the first time.
In your sweetest voice you said I should "ball"
you, shocking me with that old

obscenity from childhood. We weren't old
enough then to worry that the grass
rolling underneath us like a ball
would vanish, and the green, tipsy field,
grown sober, would dry up in time,
and the whole day turn to dust.

Now the umpire bends to dust
off the plate. "Batter up, old
man," he quips. I swing, and this time
the ball goes sailing out over the grass,
over the fielders' heads and the field,
smaller and smaller until it's nothing like a ball

until *I* am the ball and the field
and the old love in the grass
with time yet to kick up some dust.

THE POETRY LESSON

She says she has a good idea —
she will write a poem to Grandma.
She writes:
    A Poem   *by Molly*
and stops, shining in the October dusk,
stumped. "How do you write a poem?"
she asks me. "You're the poem-maker.
Tell me how." I tell her
there need be no rhyme
or reason. I tell her the fall,
or the feel of the things that she loves,
finding her words
for my bright ideas.
My wife says, "Just write
about your walk home from school."
Later, she comes back,
clutching a paper:
    On a wok hom fom scool I sow a fyre engyn.
    I poot my hand on my mauth.
I think of myself with
my love, hope, and tears,
my raft of important abstractions.
I laugh at the poem
and turn back to my daughter,
to praise her particular lights.
But she's gone.

POEM WRITTEN MOSTLY
BY FOURTH GRADERS

They're all here, exactly where we left them
so many years ago, familiar as sonnets,
the thumb-suckers and small sprawlers,
the bed wetters, best friends, and bullies,
grouped on the grade school auditorium risers
in their pigtails and crew cuts,
their headbands and braces,
their cub scout belts and tennies,
their inimitable swaggers and grins.
Here's the girl with her pants snap open,
here's the boy excavating his nose,
here's the fat kid with bottle-thick
glasses, his shirt buttoned up to his neck,
gawking at nothing at all. And yet

who are these strangers who march up one by one,
a bouquet of stiff papers clutched in their hands,
to make humpback whales wash up in Wisconsin,
dogs take ballet and play baseball and soccer,
sunfish rise and set and tell jokes under water?
Who told them that gray is a suitcase or a gray
moldy carrot, that blue doesn't argue
but despises black, that people who turn into possums
eat eggshells, that a girl, dressed in red,
reading a poem about red
and how her face turns red
when she feels foolish, turns red?
Behind me, a grandmother says, "Back in my time
these weren't called poems. They don't even rhyme!"

While beside me my five-year-old starry-eyed daughter
shouts, "That was a great one!" up to her nine-year-old sister
and brings the house down
as the air fills with dolphins of laughter,
a ripple of whistles and clicks
finning through waves of applause.
So the laws of nostalgia are broken
as our children and childhoods threaten
to sail off without and beyond us
into their own strange lands,
until the moth-eaten red curtain closes,
the thumb-suckers and sprawlers return like a tide
and we take them, small wonders, bright charms,
in the nets of our metrical arms.

TRASH-PICKING

—for Emily, age six

For weeks you've been asking for trash—
broken buttons, flip tops, and paper clips,
used Kleenex, and toilet paper rolls,
packing crates, old shoes, and light bulbs
that breed in your room down the hall.
For weeks I've been blocked up, abstracted.

Today I've been thinking how much we throw out
as inconsequential, replaceable.
How perfectly good words, even, seem to break down,
losing their useful shine,
exposing their ratchets and gears,
until, one by one, we discard them.

Now you show me your packing crate robots,
your light bulb and toilet paper dolls,
your paper clip flip-top finger puppets,
and I'm off to my wastebasket, singing
Verily! Eftsoons! Forsooth!
Here's *Beauty!* Here's *Love!* Here's *Truth!*

III. Poppies

THE SECRET OF LEVITATION

The curtain opened on the grade school stage.
Dressed in his size forty-two pants and shoes
the clown magician showed us his magic:
the rabbit in the hat, the scarves up the sleeve,
the ball in the cup—all the usual tricks.
But he'd promised to show us the secret of levitation.

I thought if I knew the secret of levitation
I'd teach it to my father. He was at that stage
of multiple sclerosis when his body was playing tricks
on him, making him trip over his shoes
or lose his large hands in his sleeves.
I was eight, and believed in magic.

What happened next that day might have been magic.
We fell silent as the clown prepared for levitation,
his body covered up on a cot, his long sleeves
and a bright blanket draped to the stage,
his red nose aimed at the ceiling, his huge shoes
stuck out awry from under the blanket. Tricks!

he laughed, placing his arms under the blanket. Tricks
are nothing compared to real magic.
The blanket began to rustle. Then his shoes
lifted off the cot. We gasped. Silence, he said. Levitation
requires absolute silence. His body rose over the stage,
swaying as effortlessly as an arm in a sleeve.

All week I'd been pulling things from my sleeves,
showing my mother and father all my small tricks,
my bed pulled out from the wall, my stage.
For my mother, anything I did was magic.
But for my father, nothing less than levitation
would do. Now, said the clown, watch my shoes.

We watched as the blanket slipped off of the shoes
stuck on horizontal poles from his outstretched sleeves.
He marched around the stage, the secret of levitation
become just another of his clever tricks.
We laughed, but something had happened to magic
that day on the grade school auditorium stage.

So, when I rose from my bedroom stage, practicing levitation,
my father's shoe-tipped crutches stuck under my foolish sleeves,
it was magic, I insisted. Magic. I didn't tell him it was only a trick.

WHO ART IN HEAVEN?

All night the poison ivy
blossoms on my rump.
I roll and scratch
in a nightmare of itch,
the sheets stiffened with seepage.
Time drifts. It's 1955. I'm ten.
Our vacation was supposed
to have ended last week,
but my father, multiple sclerosis
stripping the myelin from his spine,
is in bed with a sulfa reaction,
boils and pustules rupturing
his skin. Too weak to walk,
his crutches huddled awkward in the corner,
he grimaces or grins.
It is my job to empty
the large jar of urine
bubbling with blood and pus
into the toilet.
We don't talk much.
I wander around my grandmother's house
hating him, wondering why
I'm given this punishment.
The house is large and dark,
dusty embroidery hung on the walls:
The Lord Is My Shepherd, I Shall Not Want;
Our Father Who Art In Heaven.
The long days dawdle and sulk.
Until finally he is well,
and we're home, the nightmare over.

Now, years later, alone in the dark,
I lie here, scrubbing my rump,
festering with loss and indignity,
and God's best punchline, memory,
its blister, and itch, and burn.

BINGO

I wheel him into the dayroom,
his thin lips stiff, unhinging.
"I ain't gonna play," he complains.
"I know how, but I just ain't."
Behind us, a young woman,
legs splayed and quivering, chokes
on the air, her thin hair
lifting its wings.
Two crones in the corner
stare into their hands,
comparing their wrinkled calligraphy.
One old man lolls, helpless, confused,
wheeling himself through sleep.

The caller begins. The room fills
with the flick and clack of gameboards,
wet gums, sniff, cough, and spittle,
the shuffle of nurses and pills.
Darkness settles.
The caller collects his cards
as the players disappear,
withering into
the shadows of their small talk.
I and my father follow.
"I'm sorry," I tell him.
"I'm sorry we lost."
"Bingo!" he calls out. "Bingo!"

SECRETS

We have never been very much good
at talking, but now,
moving toward this last intractable silence,
together we try. I ask you about
your hopes and dreams, your reconciliations.
You tell me about selling strawberries
at a nickel a quart in the dusty Iowa sun,
the bullfrog hunt at Old Man Miller's pond,
the way you hung out in Peterson's Drugs
just to watch Martha Johnson's blouse droop down
as she scooped the ice cream up.
I smile and nod and don't tell you
I've heard it all before.
You ask me about my needs and feelings,
my desires and aspirations.
I tell you about cross-country skiing,
ice fishing, waxworms, and tip-ups,
the way my daughters learned to skate
in the cold Wisconsin winter.
You smile and nod and tell me
you hope everything goes well.
It grows dark, the nurses flitting
in and out of your illness
with their pills and small adjustments.
And we sit together in this awkward dusk,
silent, unsatisfied, sad,
full of secrets so familiar
we don't know what they are.

WELL

It's a deep subject, he'd say, his best joke.
And deeper: Back in an antic landscape,
closer to that slick stone edge of sickness
than any young hero could know.

And deeper: His big voice grown thinner,
slipped down in a shimmer
of multiple sclerosis,
an echo, a protest, a moan.
Whose was the broken promise?

And deeper: Only his head above water.
One leg pulled up after another
like buckets. Ensorcelled by walls,
no magical landscape, no princess,
no well, no golden balls.

THE POET, GRAVESIDE

You said that you would never want to be
remembered as anything but lucky.
But now, a year after your death, and here,
in this stark, symmetrical place more
rigid than the most restrictive poem,
I wonder whom to blame your luck on—God?

You said that you could always turn to God,
that given any situation He would be
more solace than the most respected poem.
And did I think that I was merely lucky
in my talent and accomplishment? More
likely God had put me, for some reason, here.

Still, my father, I ask why you are here.
And through those long, untimely years did God
watch your slow paralysis grow, more
deaf than He had any right to be?
I'd rather think that you were just unlucky
and not some pawn in God's unending poem.

I'd like to think that somehow my small poem
could bring a measure of solace, even here.
Whitman said he felt that death was lucky,
that he could far outstrip most any god,
that through his manly verses we could be
immortal—a self, a song, a kosmos, something more.

Soon enough, we'll all be nothing more
than figures in some unforgotten poem
(if we're lucky). *God, don't let us be
cut off, incomplete, like a sestina, ending here.*

LETTER TO MY FATHER

The children now call you Grandpa-Who-Died.
I remember them
skipping in and out of your illness
through all of their small lives,

as you slumped in your paralyzed chair,
a thin strand of spittle splitting your lips,
your discolored tooth and difficult grin,
the squint of your pale, blind eye.

I wondered what they must think of you,
clipped to your catheter sack and urine,
your hands clumped limp on your lap robe,
your legs cut off at the thigh.

Now they tell me they remember
Grandpa-Who-Died:
how he walked and ran and played with them,
how he'd skip, and wheel, and glide!

POPPIES

"I made them big because I wanted people to see them."
—Georgia O'Keeffe

Later, your death pales. That huge
gash in the canvas
shrinks back to manageable size,
leaving me only
this flower, this flat reproduction.

O'Keeffe knew
how the world falls away
in smallness,
how the grand shapes

shrivel to miniatures
pressed behind glass,
how there is no angle from which
our puny architectures won't survive.

So her poppies unbutton, voluptuous
eruptions of color, the bright
sensual canvas
raging with palpable light.

Could I make of your death such a flower,
such a terrible firestorm
of tenderness,
your death would grow large again.
Your death would not die.

IV. People and Dog in the Sun

THE JUGGLER

First it was just balls,
one, then two, then three in the air.
Then it was the children's playthings:
stuffed dogs, small dolls, a dollhouse chair.
And then his wife's things:
her pillows, utensils, her underwear.
Now he's juggling the children.
They're giggling and buoyant up in the air,
and his wife, worried, complaining,
now she's there,
and the house and the block and the city
and the world spinning. Is it
too much for him? Does he dare?
Now he's juggling the planets and galaxies,
the stars, the stars. Until
everything's falling—stars, galaxies, planets,
wife, children, and pillows,
small playthings and dolls, until
he's juggling air, in one lung, out the other,
wondering, with all his long practice,
why he can't handle it, there.

THE WORRIER

He knows instinctively
that if it can possibly happen
it will.
And yet he thinks if he just thinks
about it enough,
and expresses his grave concern,
it won't.
He knows if he doesn't worry about it
and it happens,
he'll have been caught unawares.
If he does worry and it does happen,
he will have told them so.
But mostly he thinks if he worries
it won't happen.

And so, he worries:
His walls have no pictures
lest the tacks crack the plaster
and send the walls tumbling down.
His car, seldom driven,
sits in the garage,
dressed in a fresh coat of wax.
His wife and his children
are immaculate and fragile,
rarely rumpled or touched.
Meanwhile, he sits in his room,
distant, unbudgeable,
waiting for everything to happen.
In his whole life nothing
is ever used up or broken.

"WELCOME TO THE ONLY WAUNAKEE IN THE WORLD"

Puckered with buckshot,
the old sign rusts.
Out on the edge of town,
the modest suburbs fluster the cornfields,
the rich land untended now,
the dairy farms gone sour, dried up.
On Main Street the wind leans
against the abandoned feed store,
limps past the empty cheese factory
curdling in the breeze, whistles through
Swenson's Butcher Shop and Schalle's Antiques
where two dogs snooze
through the vacant afternoons.

Midtown, the streets are empty,
the railroad tracks abandoned
or amazed by occasional trains.
Further on, a few side streets stretch out, senile,
twiddling their dusty thumbs. Down one
a broken tractor huddles in the dump,
an old hog slumbers in a barnyard,
and one lost chicken blows slowly past
the last Waunakee in the world.
On the edge of town, the power lines cluck
their unreluctant tongues,
while a stunted windmill turns and pumps
its slow, unsteady pulse.

MURDER

I.

I'm high up on the hillside, tending goats,
when the news comes, as it always does,
by phone, and your sobs
throb from the house
to lacerate the blue afternoon.
Your grandmother has been murdered.
The words stumble and burn.
The whole familiar countryside turns
alien with grief.
How could anyone do such a thing?
How could anyone do it?
We hold ourselves against her
final moments, and we weep.

II.

The police piece it together:
Roland Steele, small-time
con man, drifter, thug,
who once threw himself down
his best friend's stairs to sue him
(unfortunately, he wasn't hurt);
who, "incarcerated," as he liked to say,
(he wasn't dumb, he liked to say)
hung himself from a prison bunk bed just enough
to get moved to better quarters;
who, when the FBI let him out
to follow him to some bigger fish,
gave them the slip.
Oh, he was sly. He was quick.

III.

Quick enough to talk any old lady
out of a diamond ring for his girl friend
or a few bills for himself,
or gallantly fix the tire
he himself had slashed
on your grandmother's old Dodge Dart
and drive her out of town
and beat her slow to death
and dump her under garbage in the ditch.
Roland Steele, back in jail
(for all the good it will do us)
the only one there to hold her
when she died in his arms.

IV.

Goddamn you Roland Steele!
You son of a bitch! You bastard!
You uninvited intimate!
You enter our lives.
You are in the family album.
I want to know, Roland, did you
bugger barnyard animals in your youth?
Did you abuse your sister?
Did you damage everything you got your hands on?
If there were words strong enough
to hurt you, I would discharge an arsenal.
But there is only *murder*.
And for all my liberal talk
I want you gone.

V.

Weeks pass. The world
asserts itself. People
go on about their business
weary of old news until
there is no one left to tell.
So I'm down in the goat yard
telling the goats
about the vagaries of love,
about meaninglessness and murder,
wondering if God is satisfied
or suitably appalled.
But they are only goats.
And why should goats be expected
to understand anything at all?

NIGHTLINE:
AN INTERVIEW WITH THE GENERAL

The retired general is talking about restraint,
how he could have blown them all to kingdom come.
Read between the lines: this man's a saint.

War is, after all, not for the faint-
hearted. It's more than glory, fife, and drum,
and tired generals talking of restraint.

Make no mistake. He's never been one to paint
a rosy picture, mince words, or play dumb.
Caught behind the lines no man's a saint.

But why should strong offensives ever taint
a country pressed by Leftist, Red, and Hun?
He's generally tired of talking about restraint,

tired of being muzzled by every constraint
put on him. He thinks the time has come
to draw the line between the devil and the saint,

to silence protest, demonstration, and complaint,
beneath a smooth, efficient, military hum.
The general's retired all talk of restraint.
He aligns himself with God. And God's no saint.

GROUND ZERO

"I felt a great shriek in nature."
—Edvard Munch

He knew how everything, at extremes, is the same:
how heat freezes, joy pains;
how the most unbearable sound is silence;
how a scream turns even the firm world liquid,
a sea beyond human keening;
how the bell of the skull starts vibrating out
into the great heart of the sky;
how the dull hands are clapped
like dogs' ears to the head;
how we'd pull that head off, if only
the lake weren't its mouth,
the sky its skinned eyelids,
the night oozing in oily and woozy.

Why was it given him to hear this?
This scream of the possum-faced preener,
the simian seductress,
the sweetheart that turns all men green;
this scream of the papery matron
draped in a greatcoat of syphilis,
her raw hands mittened in flesh,
basting her naked child;
this scream of the white house drowning
in bloodfire, the gray face rolling off
of the terrified canvas,
the long tongue of the road
breaking up in intemperate paint;
this scream of lopped limbs and two-headed men
in all their ludicrous, formal dress,
as if no one must ever lose face,
as if no one were incomplete;

this scream of the murderer's
thick hands and wrists, as he twists
slightly sideways, and toward us.

Ground zero. Hairless and legless. The scream
of this whole goddamned universe squirms into us.
While somewhere above us,
safe on their bridge into space,
two blue friends walk off the deaf canvas,
as if at a certain distance,
as if in an obdurate silence,
as if toward some not unimaginable bright town.

SINBAD THE SAILOR

Sinbad is standing on top of his boat
while on top of his head grows a flower.
To his right, three comically menacing fish
glower in the failing, angular light
that grazes the tip of his spear.
Their jowls drip ketchup the color of blood.

I don't think it's meant to be real blood
any more than the pea pod boat's a real boat
or the pole vaulter's pole's a real spear.
And Sinbad himself is no more than a flower
aglow with the same inner light
that lights up and sequesters the fish.

Meanwhile, the piebald, impossible fish
for all their grotesqueness, seem Sinbad's blood
relatives. On either side of the light,
on top of the water, on top of the boat,
foolish monsters and harlequin sailor flower
the same incongruous motley. And the spear

the color of Sinbad's pantaloons is the spear
that colors the blood of the fish.
On the edge of the scene, night's a blue flower.
In the middle, the land is dark as dried blood.
It seems like they're all in the same boat,
locked in this jest of geometric light.

What does it mean to see the world in this light?
To see monsters and heroes with spears
as alike? To see men in their boats
and immense, pantalooned fish,
as the same flesh, the same blazoned blood?
What strange idea comes to flower?

In Los Alamos, the desert produces a flower
so bright its fiery petals can light
up a city, and slip into the blood
more surely than any broadsword or spear.
In that light who could tell a terrible fish
from a small faceless man in a boat?

Our heads grow such flowers! We brandish such spears!
Such fish monsters swim in our blood!
We will grow light and fall out of our planet, our boat!

MERIDA: THE MARKET

Too warm for December: the sun hung up
with the piñatas in the market;
little girls on the streetcorners, slitting
the citrus, paring their flowers of lime;
old women with bags of chili'd orange slices;
old men hacking up pig hocks and octopi;
the flavor of shoe leather, fish, avocado,
coconut, grapefruit, papaya, lemon rind.

Caught in the clothing market
hot with con men hawking their rugs,
their fake ancient carvings, "nice blouses and dresses,"
the fine handwork of the Mayan peasants,
we walk with a fast-talking mestizo:
"Cheap goods," he pleads. "Hear me out, gringo.
Give me one moment of your time."

He lovingly lays out his dresses,
shows us the stitching, the fine quality weave,
quotes us a price we should know is too high,
but we watch as he pinches our 5,000 peso note,
as if he's ashamed just to hold it,
and, looking us straight in the eye,
says, "See, I shine my shoes with it."
Now what else would we like to buy?

And so we are taken, as, under the snickering sky,
we walk back through the fish and fruit stalls,
back past the pig hocks, orange slices, and lime,
back past the bright, unlikely piñatas,
the *pescadoes, jaguares, quetzals, cochinos,*
the sun shattered over the market, scattering
its gifts in this land's broken light.

SEASIDE, COZUMEL

Across the road a squat mestizo holds
a snarling armadillo by the tail.
Behind them, buzzards hump the roadside dump.
A squashed iguana contemplates the pave.

The jungle says nothing. Give it a month
and it would take it all back,
claim it was all a mistake.
It should never have let go so lightly.

Slumped in our own blue funk,
we slosh into the water
graceless in face masks and flippers,
one with the chubs, groupers, and grunts.

Until the sea takes us in,
and slowly the day makes way
for angelfish, yellow stripe,
fan coral and conch.

And we are the fly in the amber,
and we are the sand in the pearl,
and we are the intentional flaw in the rug
that even a god could find beautiful.

AT HALF-MOON BAY

These gold hills. Everywhere
there is money.

Now on the freeway,
out from the ransomed houses,
beyond the cedar shake and stucco,
far from the greenback lawns,
even this land, reclaimed from sand dunes
in 1902, oleander, redwood, eucalyptus, and palm,
continues the fable of water.

Slumming at the Fish Trap Restaurant.
Deep-fried calamari and rockfish,
saltwater perch and prawns,
this rich harvest.
Who'd have imagined
so much from sea wrack and sand?

And if this currency were gone?
The sprinklers and pumps shut down,
the aquifers filled with the sea,
tidepools of mussels and stars?

Somewhere in South Dakota,
outside his rocky trailer,
an old man stands watering
his windfall of hollyhocks
in a porcelain toilet bowl planter.
While here, on this rich night,
an old fisherman out on the breakwater
opens his wonderful bucket:
half-moons and silver dollars.

PEOPLE AND DOG IN THE SUN

Summer: to the lakefront the old people
come, walking their whimsical dogs.
Each year when the sentimental sun
comes back to admire its face in the water,
these twosomes return: the old
story of loneliness and love. And each time

I see them, awkwardly rocking in time
to the same broken song, they seem less like people
than like strange haunted vessels—old
boats that all winter have gone to the dogs
until now, here, beside the bright water,
they drift in the westering sun.

"There's nothing new under the sun,"
one of them tells me this time.
"You'd think they could walk on water,"
she goes on about those "terrible people"
who think they're her betters, who continually dog
the poor, the unfortunate, the old.

And I wonder what it's like to be old
in this country: A meandering walk in the sun,
some small talk in the company of a dog
one's last best hope of a good time.
I think how different it must be for these people
so near death, their names written on water.

Such thoughts, I know, won't hold water.
Most ways, I suppose, even the very old
are like anyone else. People are people.
No matter the season, the sun is the sun.
And further, there is something about the times
hanging around us *all* like an old dog,

some dark, irremediable hunger. Miro's dog
dreams a man from its head, the gray air thick as water.
His small boy blaring by is a clock racing time,
his woman a mushroom that will never grow old,
his whole portrait the color of the sun.
What do we make of these people?

If time disappears in a fury of sun,
if we all, old and young, become so much vaporized water,
may some sly dog live on, whimsically dreaming up people.

PITT POETRY SERIES
Ed Ochester, General Editor

Dannie Abse, *Collected Poems*
Claribel Alegría, *Flowers from the Volcano*
Jon Anderson, *Death and Friends*
Jon Anderson, *In Sepia*
Jon Anderson, *Looking for Jonathan*
Maggie Anderson, *Cold Comfort*
John Balaban, *After Our War*
Michael Benedikt, *The Badminton at Great Barrington; Or, Gustave Mahler & the Chattanooga Choo-Choo*
Michael Burkard, *Ruby for Grief*
Kathy Callaway, *Heart of the Garfish*
Siv Cedering, *Letters from the Floating World*
Lorna Dee Cervantes, *Emplumada*
Robert Coles, *A Festering Sweetness: Poems of American People*
Kate Daniels, *The White Wave*
Norman Dubie, *Alehouse Sonnets*
Stuart Dybek, *Brass Knuckles*
Odysseus Elytis, *The Axion Esti*
Brendan Galvin, *The Minutes No One Owns*
Gary Gildner, *Blue Like the Heavens: New & Selected Poems*
Gary Gildner, *Digging for Indians*
Gary Gildner, *First Practice*
Gary Gildner, *Nails*
Gary Gildner, *The Runner*
Bruce Guernsey, *January Thaw*
Michael S. Harper, *Song: I Want a Witness*
Gwen Head, *The Ten Thousandth Night*
Barbara Helfgott Hyett, *In Evidence: Poems of the Liberation of Nazi Concentration Camps*
Milne Holton and Graham W. Reid, eds., *Reading the Ashes: An Anthology of the Poetry of Modern Macedonia*
Milne Holton and Paul Vangelisti, eds., *The New Polish Poetry: A Bilingual Collection*
David Huddle, *Paper Boy*
Lawrence Joseph, *Shouting at No One*
Shirley Kaufman, *From One Life to Another*
Shirley Kaufman, *Gold Country*
Etheridge Knight, *The Essential Etheridge Knight*
Ted Kooser, *One World at a Time*
Ted Kooser, *Sure Signs: New and Selected Poems*
Larry Levis, *Winter Stars*
Larry Levis, *Wrecking Crew*

Robert Louthan, *Living in Code*
Tom Lowenstein, tr., *Eskimo Poems from Canada and Greenland*
Archibald MacLeish, *The Great American Fourth of July Parade*
Peter Meinke, *Night Watch on the Chesapeake*
Peter Meinke, *Trying to Surprise God*
Judith Minty, *In the Presence of Mothers*
Carol Muske, *Camouflage*
Carol Muske, *Wyndmere*
Leonard Nathan, *Carrying On: New & Selected Poems*
Leonard Nathan, *Dear Blood*
Leonard Nathan, *Holding Patterns*
Kathleen Norris, *The Middle of the World*
Sharon Olds, *Satan Says*
Alicia Ostriker, *The Imaginary Lover*
Greg Pape, *Black Branches*
Greg Pape, *Border Crossings*
James Reiss, *Express*
William Pitt Root, *Faultdancing*
Liz Rosenberg, *The Fire Music*
Dennis Scott, *Uncle Time*
Herbert Scott, *Groceries*
Richard Shelton, *Of All the Dirty Words*
Richard Shelton, *Selected Poems, 1969-1981*
Richard Shelton, *You Can't Have Everything*
Arthur Smith, *Elegy on Independence Day*
Gary Soto, *Black Hair*
Gary Soto, *The Elements of San Joaquin*
Gary Soto, *The Tale of Sunlight*
Gary Soto, *Where Sparrows Work Hard*
Tomas Tranströmer, *Windows & Stones: Selected Poems*
Chase Twichell, *Northern Spy*
Chase Twichell, *The Odds*
Constance Urdang, *The Lone Woman and Others*
Constance Urdang, *Only the World*
Ronald Wallace, *People and Dog in the Sun*
Ronald Wallace, *Tunes for Bears to Dance To*
Cary Waterman, *The Salamander Migration and Other Poems*
Bruce Weigl, *A Romance*
David Wojahn, *Glassworks*
David P. Young, *The Names of a Hare in English*
Paul Zimmer, *Family Reunion: Selected and New Poems*